Joseph C. Wallace

Wallace's Street and City Guide of Albany

Price Twenty-Five Cents.

WALLACE'S STREET AND CITY GUIDE OF ALBANY.

PRESENTED BY

JOSEPH C. WALLACE,

Advertising Agent and Publisher,

505 BROADWAY,

(Office of J. W. Kiernan, Insurance Agent.)

☞ See inside Back Cover ☜

WALLACE'S

Street and City Guide,

OF

ALBANY.

A COMPLETE GUIDE FOR THE CITIZEN AND STRANGER

TO ITS

PUBLIC BUILD'GS,

Churches,

CEMETERIES,

ETC.

RAILROADS,

Steamboats,

LODGES,

ETC.

WITH STREET DIRECTORY.

SPRING—1870.—No. 3.

Published by Joseph C. Wallace, Albany, N. Y.

Charles Van Benthuysen & Sons' Print, Albany.

1

THE

TWEDDLE HALL

DOLLAR STORE

OF ALBANY.

One of the Principal Places of Interest and Profit
to Visitors in the City.

A MAGNIFICENT SALESROOM !

Furnished with one hundred and forty feet in length of
full White Metal Show Cases.

AN IMMENCE STOCK

Of **BEAUTIFUL and DESIRABLE ARTICLES,**
in great variety, representing nearly every kind of business.

POLITE AND ATTENTIVE YOUNG LADIES !

Will show every attention to Visitors.

The Tweddle Hall Dollar Store,

83 State St., Albany.

ALBANY

FIRE ALARM TELEGRAPH.

---

2. Green and Nucella.
3. Green and Arch.
4. Taylor's Brewery.
5. Green and Herkimer.
6. B'way and Madison ave.
7. Hamilton and Union.
8. Broadway and Hudson.
9. State and Green.
12. S. Pearl and Schuyler.
13. Morton and Grand.
14. S. Pearl and Westerlo.
15. Madison Av. and Pearl.
16. Madison Av. and Philip.
17. South Pearl and Plain.
18. Grand and Beaver.
19. South Pearl and State.
21. De Witt and Montgomery.
23. North Ferry and Water.
24. N. Ferry and Broadway.
25. R. R. Crossing & B'dway.
26. Lumber and Water.
27. Broadway & Clinton Av.
28. Broadway and Columbia.
29. B'dway & Maiden Lane.
31. N. Pearl and Van Woert.
32. N. Pearl and Lumber.
34. Monroe and Chapel.

35. Orange and Swan.
36. Canal and Hawk.
37. Canal and North Pearl.
38. Lodge and Pine.
39. Eagle and State.
41. Wash. Av. and Hawk.
42. Lancaster and Hawk.
43. State and Swan.
45. Lancaster and Dove.
46. Wash. Av. and Dove.
51. Central Av. and Knox.
52. Wash. Av. and Snipe.
53. Bradford and Robin.
54. Central Av. and Perry.
61. Eagle and Hudson
62. Eagle and Elm
63. Hamilton and Hawk.
64. Madison Av. and Swan.
65. Jefferson and Dove.
71. Madison Av. and Lark.
72. Penitentiary.
73. Alms House.
74. Paigeville.
81. Clin. Av. and Ten Broeck.
82. Second and Swan.
83. Lumber and Swan.
84. Third and Lark.

Maurice E. Viele,

IMPORTER

And Wholesale and Retail Dealer in

English, French, German & American

HARDWARE

AND

CUTLERY.

ALSO,

Swedes, English & American

BAR and BUNDLE IRON,

Tin Plates, Copper and Zinc.

NOS. 41 & 43 STATE STREET,

ALBANY, N. Y.

GENERAL INDEX.

INDEX TO PATRONS.

Bathing Suits made to order at John E. Page's Gent's Furnishing Store and Custom Shirt Manufactory, 462 and 464 Broadway.

Joseph C. Wallace

Wallace's Street and City Guide of Albany

ISBN/EAN: 9783337020484

Printed in Europe, USA, Canada, Australia, Japan

Cover: Foto ©Andreas Hilbeck / pixelio.de

More available books at **www.hansebooks.com**

CHINA

Tea Store

No. 1 Beaver Block,

Corner of Norton & South Pearl Streets.

TEAS, COFFEES,

Spices and Sugars,

WHOLESALE AND RETAIL,

A. N. BRADY, Prop'r.

Historical Sketch of Albany,

A LBANY was known by the several Dutch names of
   BEAVER-WYCK WILLIAMSTADT and FORT ORANGE,
chiefly by the latter. The lands immediately opposite to
Albany, and for a distance along and from the river, the
Dutch denoted as HET GREENE BOSH, the *pine woods*, cor-
rupted to *Greenbush*.

Albany city may be said to have been founded in 1612, by
some Hollanders, and to have been, next to Jamestown, Va.,
the earliest European settlement within the primitive thirteen
United States. A temporary fort was erected in 1614, and
Fort Orange in 1623. By that name it was known until after
the British conquest, in 1664, when it received the name of
Albany from one of the titles of the Duke of York.

The change of sovereignty which the colony of New Netherland underwent in 1664, necessarily interfered with the
language as well as the customs and manners of the people.

The records continued, for twenty years after that event,
to be written mostly in Dutch; but, in 1686, they were
required to be kept in English. The Dutch was the oral language of the city for many years after.

In 1629 a charter of liberties and exemptions for patroons,
masters and private individuals who should plant colonies
in New Netherland was granted by the States General of
Holland. At the time the charter was granted Albany presented the appearance of a small town, with two principal
streets crossing each other, in one of which was placed all
the public buildings. (This no doubt accounts for the great
width of State street.) It had a very rural appearance, each
house having its garden and shade trees. There were three
docks, the lower, middle and upper ; the lower was called
the king's dock. Vessels were unloaded by the aid of canoes
lashed together, and having a platform built upon them
where goods were placed.

Under this charter, in August, 1630, Kilaen Van Rensselaer
purchased through his agents a large tract of land, including
most of this as well as several of the adjacent counties. In
1631, he sent a colony and gave it the name of Rensselaer-

HUMPHREY'S DRUG STORE.

CARD.—Having this day sold out my entire stock of Drugs, Medicines, Paints, Oils, Glass, Druggists' Sundries and Fancy Goods, to JOHN J. St. JOHN, I take this opportunity to tender my sincere thanks to my friends for the patronage bestowed on me for so many years, and most respectfully solicit a continuance of the same for my successor.

ALBANY, March 1, 1870. **JOHN R. HUMPHREY.**

JOHN J. St. JOHN,

Wholesale and Retail Dealer in

DRUGS, MEDICINES,

PAINTS, OILS, GLASS,

Druggists' Sundries and Fancy Goods,

39 WASHINGTON AVENUE,

ALBANY, N. Y.

wyck, after changed to Beaverwick. In 1643 the first church was erected. Albany was fortified against the Indians by the Dutch with a stockade in 1645, and vestiges of the work remained until 1812. The city was incorporated by the Colonial Governor Dongan, in 1686, with an area one mile wide on the river, extending northwest to the north line of the manor of the Rensselaers, and retaining that width thirteen and a half miles.

During the revolutionary war the city presented a singular appearance ; it was stockaded, had its north and south gates, was an important military post, and was commanded by the gallant Lafayette and Col. Van Schaick, a distinguished officer and a native of Albany. It was considered one of the most important stations in the United States. It was the key to the north and west, the point from which our armies threatened Montreal and Quebec.

Albany nobly sustained their countrymen in their opposition to British sway, and afforded aid in troops and money to the suffering inhabitants of Tyron county to assist them in repelling the frequent attacks of the merciless hordes of Tories and Indians who ravaged that settlement.

Burgoyne had boasted at the commencement of the campaign that his army would revel upon the spoils of Albany, but he only visited the city as a captive. Sir Henry Clinton twice attempted to invade but met with sufficient obstacles to prevent his success. It became the capitol of the State in 1807. Its bounds were enlarged by addition of part of the small town of Colonie, 25th of February, 1815, which formerly formed the Fifth Ward; area 7160 acres. The city lies in 42 deg. 39 min. 3 sec. N. Lat., and 30 deg. 12 min. E. Long. from Washington, and is distant from New York 142 miles, Boston 200 miles, and Buffalo 298 miles.

The plat on which the city lies is uneven, a low alluvial flat extends along the river from 15 to 100 rods wide, west of which rises a hill of clay and sand. In the one-half mile 153 feet, and in the next about 67 feet high from the summit. The county is an even plain for miles.

The city appears to great advantage from the river, rising rapidly from the bank, and exhibiting its public buildings in bold relief. The public buildings are many of them elegant and costly, and are fully described in another part of this book.

Since the introduction of steamboats and the completion of canals, the growth of the city and county has been rapid.

The old portion of the city is not remarkable for the regularity of its streets, but the modern has more symmetery. In 1845 the city had but 116 streets ; it now contains about 180. The principal of which are State, Broadway, North and South Pearl streets and Washington avenue. The city con-

" HAINES,"

PHOTOGRAPHER

478 BROADWAY,

(Opposite Stanwix Hall.)

Photography in all its Branches.

Portraits, Views and Interiors,

ENLARGING

AND FINISHING IN

Oil, Water Color, or India Ink.

Also, Printing for the Trade, of Sculpture,
Paintings, Engravings, &c., both by
Contact and Solar Process, at
Lowest Market Rates.

PHOTOGRAPHS OF THE NEW CAPITAL.

Publisher of

Stereoscopes of Morbid Specimens

FOR THE

MEDICAL PROFESSION.

tains many public institutions of learning and benevolence. The people are principally engaged in manufacturing and commerce, which are varied and extensive.

Albany is the largest lumber market in the State.

At the junction of the Erie canal with the Hudson river, the citizens have constructed an extensive basin to protect the boats from the winds and give the greater facilities for discharging their cargo.

March 16th, 1870, the charter was amended enlarging its bounds by adding part of the towns of Bethlehem and Watervliet, and increasing the number of wards from 10 to 16.

From the above description a pretty clear idea can be formed of what Albany was in olden times. What Albany is now is told in the fixed facts which surround her.

It was not then surrounded by six or seven railroads, branching out in every direction and communicating with the most distant as well as the largest marts of trade, at the head of the navigation of the Hudson river, at the foot of the navigation of the Erie canal, thus forming a connecting link between the great West and the South and East, filled with manufacturing establishments of every kind, within a few hours ride of the great commercial emporium of the western world, and supplied with all the modern facilities to aid and forward the requirements of trade and commerce.

This is what Albany is now, and exhibits her as in the most flourishing condition.

—*Compiled from Munsell's Annals of Albany.*

Census of the City at Different Periods.

Year.	Population.
1790	3,498
1800	5,289
1810	10,762
1814	11,680
1820	12,630
1825	15,971
1830	24,209
1835	28,109
1840	33,721
1845	42,139
1850	50,763
1855	57,333
1860	62,367
1865	62,613
1870	80,000

STATE CAPITOL.

The State House is beautifully located on Eagle street, facing State, 130 feet above the Hudson, and has in front a

H. R. WATSON,
No. 8 Plain Street, Albany,

GENERAL UPHOLSTERY,

FRENCH
LACE CURTAINS

A SPECIALITY.

WINDOW SHADES OF ALL KINDS,

MATTRESSES

Of Curled Hair, Husk, &c.,

SPRING UNDER BEDS

Of my own Manufacture.

" THE BEST IN USE."

PRIME LIVE GEESE FEATHERS

Park of three acres, inclosed by an iron fence and planted with ornamental shade trees. The present bulding was begun in 1803 and finished in 1807, at a cost exceeding $120,000. It is built of stone, faced with Nyack red free stone, 90 feet broad, 50 feet high, and was originally 115 feet long, In 1854, fifteen feet were added to the west end. The eastern front has an Ionic portico, with four columns of Berkshire marble each 3 feet 8 inches in diameter and 33 feet high. The entrance hall is 40 by 50 feet and 16 feet high, the ceiling of which is supported by a double row of reeded columns, and the floor is vaulted and laid with squares of Italian marble. Upon the north side of the hall are the office of the Adjutant-General and the Assembly Library, and on the south side the Executive Chambers. The inner Executive Chamber has a full sized portrait of General La Fayette, painted when he was in the city in 1825. The remainder of the first story is devoted to the Assembly Chamber. The Chamber is 56 by 65 feet, and 28 feet high. Upon the east side is a gallery, supported by iron pillars, for spectators. The ceiling is richly ornamented in stucco. Over the Speaker's seat is a full length portrait of Washington. In the second story, over the entrance hall, is the Senate Chamber, 40 by 50 feet, and 22 feet high. It contains the portraits of Governor Clinton and Columbus. Over the Assembly lobbies is the room of the Court of Appeals. The Court room contains portraits of Chancellors Lansing, Sanford, Jones and Walworth, Chief Justice Spencer, Abraham Van Vechten and Daniel Cady.

The roof of the State House is pyramidal, and from the centre rises a circular cupola 20 feet in diameter, supporting a hemispherical dome upon 8 insulated Ionic columns. Upon the dome stands a wooden statue of Themis, 11 feet high, holding in her right hand a sword and in her left a balance. The Senate and Assembly begin their sessions on the 1st Tuesday of January of each year, remaining in session 100 days. Visitors admitted to Senate and Assembly Chambers only during sessions of the Legislature.

STATE HALL.

This edifice, located on Eagle street, fronting the Academy Park, may be regarded as one of the finest specimens of architectural beauty in the city. It is built of white cut stone, with a colonnade in front, supported by six ionic columns, and is surmounted by a dome. The building is 138 by 88 feet, and 65 feet high. The ceilings of the basement and of the two principal stories are groined arches, and all the rooms, excepting in the attic story, are fire proof. The basement and attic are each 19 feet, and the two principal stories each 22 feet high. It was finished in 1842, at a cost of

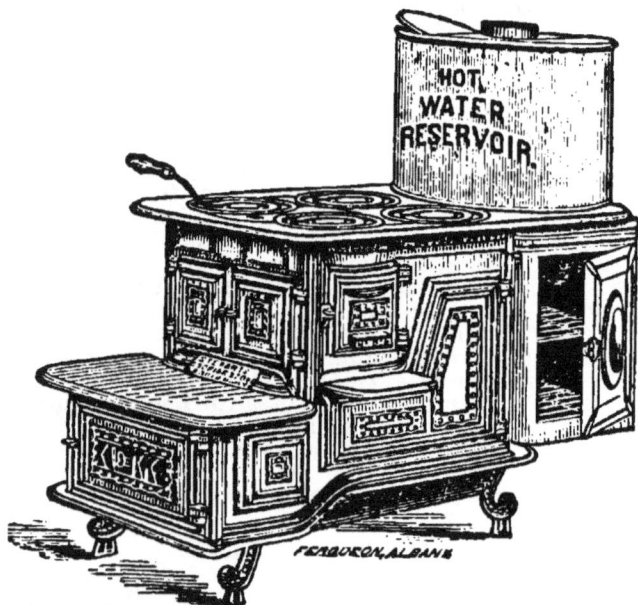

$350,000. It contains the offices of the Secretary of State; Comptroller, Treasurer, Auditor of Canal Department, Cana Appraisers, Canal Commissioners, State Engineer and Sur' veyor, Division Engineers, Clerk of Court of Appeals, Superintendent of Public Instruction, Superintendent of Bank Department, Attorney-General and State Sealer of Weights and Measures. Opened to visitors during business hours.

CITY HALL.

This edifice, situated on Eagle street fronting Washington avenue, is a fine Grecian structure of white Sing Sing marble, built at a cost of about $90,000. It is 109 feet front by 80 feet deep. In front it has a recessed porch supported by six ionic columns. In the center of the hall in the second story is a statue of Hamilton, and in the common council room are portraits of the Ex-Governors of the State. Opened to visitors during business hours. The Jail is located in rear of the City Hall, on Maiden lane.

NEW CITY BUILDING.

CITY OFFICES.

This edifice, erected by the city in the fall and winter of 1868, '69, at a cost of $200,000, occupies the site of the old center market on South Pearl street corner of Howard.

It is a beautiful structure of the Lombardic style of architecture, ornamented with a Mansard roof, and is built of brick faced with lime stone from Lake Champlain. The· first floor is occupied by the Fire and Police Commissioners, the Second Precinct Station and Overseer of the Poor. The second story contains the Police Court, Justice's Court, offices of the Assessors, Excise Commissioners and City Attorney. The third as headquarters of the Albany Fire Alarm Telegraph and Park Commissioners. Opened to visitors daily (Sundays excepted).

STATE ARSENAL.

The State arsenal was formerly located on Broadway, corner Lawrence ; was, by act of April 17, 1858, exchanged with the city for the present site on Eagle, corner Hudson. The present edifice was erected in the same year, and is of substantial workmanship and elegant architectural style. It is well supplied with arms and military equipments belonging to the State. The upper rooms are devoted to an armory.

STATE GEOLOGICAL AND AGRICULTURAL HALL.

This institution, located corner of State and Lodge streets, the site of the old State Hall, was erected in 1855, and opened to the public February 22, 1858. The building is of brick, four stories high, besides the basement. In the rear is a spacious wing, of the same height as the main building. It contains a lecture room, the spacious Geological Cabinet and the rooms of the State Geological Society. A series of English fossils have been given to the State by the British Government, and a valuable collection of shells, embracing several thousand species, has been recently presented and arranged by Philip P. Carpenter, an English naturalist. The Museum is designed to embrace a complete representation of the geological formations of the State, with their accompaning minerals and fossils. The birds and quadrupeds are preserved by a skillful taxidermist, with the attitude and appearance of life; and the reptiles and fishes are principally preserved in alcohol. Connected with this Cabinet is a historical and antiquarian department, embracing numerous aboriginal antiquities of specimens of modern Indian art, relics of battle fields, and other object of historical interest. The museum of the State Agricultural Society, in a separate department of the building, contains a large collections of obsolete and modern implements of husbandry, specimens of agricultural and mechanical products, models of fruits, samples of grains, drawings illustrating subjects connected with the useful arts, and it is designed to include an extensive collection of insects, made with special reference to showing their influence on fruit and grain crops of the State.

The whole of these collections are opened free to the public on every week day, except holidays, from 9 A. M. until 5 P. M.

THE BUREAU OF MILITARY STATISTICS.

This institution, located at 219 State street, contains flags, trophies and relics relating to the Revolution, the War of 1812, the Mexican War and the late Rebellion, forming the most complete and interesting collection ever brought together in the United States. The most deeply interesting objects perhaps are the numerous regimental flags which have been carried by our brave volunteers upon so many bloody battle fields during the late rebellion. There are also deposited many emblems of various kinds captured from the rebels by New York regiments. Inscribed on these banners are the names of the battles in which the regiments were

engaged. Upon some of them there may be found as many as seventy different inscriptions. These sad memorials of the brave dead who have fallen in the cause of liberty must ever be venerated by those who love their country and sympathized with it in its gigantic struggle for freedom. There are also many oil paintings, photographs, engravings and drawings of distinguished officers and privates. The collection of memorials increases rapidly by means of constant contributions from soldiers and their friends.

The Bureau is opened daily (except Sundays) from 9 A. M. until 5 P. M., free to all, and is visited daily by scores of strangers. Since last year as many as 20,000 persons have visited the building.

NEW YORK STATE LIBRARY.

This valuable institution, adjoining the Capitol, on State street, was founded by act of the Legislature in 1818.

For nearly thirty years the Library increased but slowly, when, in 1844, it was transferred to the Trusteeship of the Regents of the University. The present edifice of brown free stone, fronting on State street, was built in 1853, and is 114 feet long by 47 feet wide. It is a fire-proof structure, capable of accommodating 100,000 volumes. The flooring throughout is laid with encaustic tiles, and it is lighted with 180 gas burners.

The cost of the building, including land and shelving for the books, was $91,000. The Library is in two departments, containing in the aggregate 78,000 volumes. The Law Library, on the lower floor, contains 20,000 volumes, including the Laws, Journals and Documents of every State in the Union.

The General Library, in the upper story, contains about 60,000 volumes. The average annual rate of increase is about 2,500 volumes, by means of appropriations from the Legislature, donations and exchanges. Among the objects of especial interest contained in it, may be mentioned oil paintings and busts of Governors of the State, and other distinguished citizens; collections of coins, medals and engravings; the September Emancipation proclamation of President Lincoln, in his own handwriting; the original papers which Major Andre was carrying in his boot from Arnold to General Clinton, and the manuscripts of Sir Wm. Johnson and Governor George Clinton, in about twenty-five folio volumes each.

The Library is opened to the public daily from 9 A. M. until 5 P. M., and during the sessions of the Legislature until 6 P. M. All persons may read and consult the books in the Library by applying to the Librarians.

DUDLEY OBSERVATORY.

This institution, located on an eminence in the north part of the city, was founded through the munificence of Mrs. Blandina Dudley and other liberal patrons of science. It is built in the form of a cross, and was dedicated August 28th, 1856. Its management is intrusted to fifteen trustees. The building is admirably arranged and furnished with instruments, several of which are the largest and most delicate ever constructed. Among the instruments is a calculating engine made by C. Scheutz, a Swede, and purchased by John F. Rathbone. It is the only one in existence. A large class of calculations is performed by its use, and the results are impressed upon leaden plate ready to electrotype and print. It has a special library of 1,000 volumes. Admission gained by applying to the trustees.

YOUNG MEN'S ASSOCIATION FOR MUTUAL IMPROVEMENT.

This institution, located at No. 40 State street, was formed in 1833 and incorporated March 12, 1835, and was the first institution of its kind in the State for the purpose of establishing and maintaining a library, reading rooms, literary and scientific lectures, and other means of promoting moral and intellectual improvement.

Their present building of brown free stone was built in 1849, '50, and is 70 feet long by 50 feet wide, fire proof, and capable of containing 12,000 volumes. It contains a lecture room, library and reading room. The library contains 11,615 volumes. The reading room is supplied with 94 newspapers and periodicals. Its rooms are open daily to members and to strangers introduced by members. The terms of membership are an annual payment of $2.

STATE NORMAL SCHOOL.

This institution was established May 7, 1844, for the instruction and practice of teachers of common schools in the science of education and the art of teaching. Each county in the State is entitled to send twice as many pupils to the school as it sends members to the Assembly. The pupils receive tuition and the use of text books free. Males are admitted at eighteen and females at sixteen years of age. The present building, of brick, located on Lodge street, corner of Howard, was erected in 1848, at a cost of $25,000.

ALBANY ACADEMY.

This institution, for the education of boys, was chartered by the Regents March 4, 1813. The corner stone of the

present building was laid July 29, 1815, and was opened for students September 1, 1817. The building is an imposing structure of red Nyack free stone, in the Italian style, built at a cost of $100,000. It fronts on Eagle street, opposite the State Hall, and has a beautiful park of three acres, surrounded by a substantial iron fence, and planted with ornamental trees. The Academy is in a flourishing condition.

ALBANY FEMALE ACADEMY.

This institution, one of the oldest in the country for the education of females, was established in 1814, and incorporated in 1821. The present building, located at No. 28 North Pearl street, was completed May 12, 1834, and is a chaste marble building, built in Grecian style, with an Ionic portico, at a cost of $30,000.

MEDICAL COLLEGE.

This institution, located on Eagle street, between Lancaster and Jay, was incorporated February 16, 1839. Two courses of lectures annually, and the institution has secured a deservedly high reputation in the medical profession. It has an extensive medical museum opened daily to the public, free.

Attached to the College is the Law School of the University of Albany. This school was instituted under the University Charter of April 17, 1851. Two courses of lectures are annually held in rooms attached to the Medical College building.

ALBANY CITY HOSPITAL.

This institution, located on Eagle street, was incorporated April 11, 1849. It was founded by private subscription, and the present building (erected and formerly used by the city as a jail) was opened for reception of patients August 8, 1854, at a cost of $50,000. It is capable of accommodating 250 patients.

ALBANY ORPHAN ASYLUM.

This institution, located on Robin street and Western avenue, was incorporated March 30, 1831. It was commenced as a private enterprise, and the present building was erected by subscription. It is now supported by funds received from the State.

ST. VINCENT ORPHAN ASYLUM.
MALE AND FEMALE.

This institution was incorporated in 1849. The female department, situated on North Pearl street, is under the

3

S. SWEET'S

REAL ESTATE

—AND—

Insurance Agency,

532 Broadway, (Near the Two Big Trees.) Albany, N.Y.

☞ Real Estate in this city, and other parts of this and other States, such as Dwellings, Stores and other City Buildings, Vacant Lots, Country Seats, Cottages, Mills, Water Powers.

A Large Variety of Farms and Lands for Sale

OR EXCHANGE, located in this and most of the other States, North and South, East and West, including large tracts of the most valuable Mineral and Timber Lands. Also,

Examination of Titles, Conveyancing, &c.

Houses Rented & Rents Collected.

Also, Insurance Effected in Sound, Reliable Companies, on Lives, and on all description of Buildings, including Mills and Factories of all kinds, Detached Dwellings and Farm Buildings, Stock, Utensils, &c., insured from three to five years in first class Stock Companies, at low rates and free from assessments. Also, will give prompt attention to the adjustment of Insurance Claims, Fire and Inland.

charge of the Sisters of Charity. The male department, two miles west of the Capitol on the Western turnpike, is under the care of the Christian Brothers.

ALMS-HOUSE.

This institution, located on the plank road in the western part of the city, is entirely owned and managed by the city authorities. It consists of a poor-house, insane asylum (built at an expense of $12,000, and with accommodations for 80 inmates), and a fever hospital (at a cost of $5,000) ; it has a farm of 116 acres. Visitors are admitted on Thursdays only.

ALBANY COUNTY PENITENTIARY.

The Penitentiary is a fine building, located in the western part of the city, standing a little southwest of Madison avenue and Lark street. Persons convicted of certain crimes, and sentenced to short terms of imprisonment, are confined here ; and prisoners are received from Dutchess, Columbia, Rensselaer, Washington, Saratoga, Schenectady and other counties.

The Penitentiary was built in 1845, '46, and opened for prisoners in April, 1846. It was organized under the direction of its present superintendent, Amos Pilsbury, in 1848. It has 300 cells, and the average number in confinement has been 220. The convicts are principally employed in the manufacture of shoes, &c. It is opened daily to visitors, a small fee being charged for admission.

EXCHANGE BUILDING—POST OFFICE.

The Albany Exchange, a massive granite building, is situated on Broadway, occupying the entire block bounded by State, Exchange and Dean streets. It was erected in 1839, by a joint stock company, and contains the Post Office and a variety of other offices and stores.

CHURCHES.

Baptist.

First Baptist.................... Hudson corner Phillip.
North Pearl street Baptist ..... 28 North Pearl.
Calvary Baptist................ State corner High.
Tabernacle Baptist .... North Pearl above Wilson.
German Baptist................ Washington ave. near Lark.

Congregational.
First Congregational .... Eagle corner Beaver.
Congregational, Parretville ... Shaker Road.

Episcopal.
St. Peter's .... State corner Lodge.
St. Paul's .... Lancaster above Hawk.
Trinity .... Broad below Madison ave.
Church of the Holy Innocents. North Pearl corner Colonie.
Grace .... Washington ave. cor. Lark.
St. Paul's Mission Chapel...... Madison avenue.

Evangelical.
Evangelical German Asso'n... Clinton corner Nucella.
German Evan. Prot. Church... Clinton corner Alexander.

Friends.
Friends' Meeting House .... Plain near Grand.

Jewish.
Beth Jacob Synagogue .... Fulton above Madison ave.
Beth El Synagogue .... Ferry corner Franklin.
Anshe Emeth Synagogue...... South Pearl opp. Herkimer.

Lutheran.
Evang'l Lutheran Ebenezer ... Pine corner Lodge.
First German Evan. Lutheran. Nucella corner Franklin.
Second German Evan. Luth.... State above Swan.
Evan. Luth. St. John's German Central avenue.

Methodist.
Hudson street M. E. .... Hudson above Grand.
Garretson Statton M. E. .... N. Pearl above Columbia.
Ash Grove M. E............... Westerlo corner Broad.
Trinity M. E. .... Washington ave. cor. Swan.
Arbor Hill M. E............... Swan near Lumber.
Broadway M. E. .... 867 Broadway.
Sec. Wes. M. Chapel (African) Third below Lark.
African M. E................... 351 Hamilton.

Presbyterian.
First Presbyterian............. Philip corner Hudson.
Second Presbyterian .... Chapel above Maiden Lane.
Third Presbyterian ....:...... North Pearl cor. Clinton ave.
Fourth Presbyterian.......... Broadway near Wilson.
Fifth Presbyterian............ Second below Lark.

State street Presbyterian ...... State above Swan.
United Presbyterian .... Lancaster above Eagle.

Reformed Dutch.

First Reformed Prot. Dutch ... North Pearl corner Orange.
Second Reformed Prot. Dutch. Hudson below South Pearl.
Third Reformed Prot. Dutch .. Ferry corner Green.
Fourth Ref. Prot. Dutch (Ger.) Schuyler below South Pearl.
Holland Reformed Prot. Dutch Orange corner Chapel.
Park Chapel .... Hudson corner Lark.

Roman Catholic.

Cathedral, Immac. Conception Eagle corner Madison ave.
St. Mary's..................... Lodge corner Pine.
St. John's..................... Ferry corner Dallius.
St. Ann's..................... Nucella corner Franklin.
St. Joseph's.................. Ten Broeck corner Second.
St. Patrick's .... Central ave. corner Perry.
Church of Holy Cross (Ger.) .. Hamilton corner Philip.
Our Lady of the Angels (Ger.) Central avenue cor. Robin.
Blessed Virgin Mary (French). 109 Hamilton.

CEMETERIES.

ALBANY RURAL CEMETERY.

Situated on the Troy road, about midway between Albany and Troy; was established in the year 1844. It stands fifth in order of establishment of the Rural Cemeteries in the United States.

For beauty of natural scenery it far surpasses Greenwood. Its monuments are not as costly, yet for beauty of design and finish, there are few can excel. Among the magnificent monuments in this Cemetery, may be mentioned the Bank's memorial. The base of dark granite, the body of lighter granite, surmounted by a large marble statue, representing the "Angel at the Sepulchre," executed by Palmer. It stands near the south limits of the grounds. The Rensselaer and Saratoga railroad runs through the grounds. It is also accessible by Albany and West Troy Horse cars.

ST. AGNES' CEMETERY.

This Cemetery, located on the Troy road, adjoining the Albany Rural Cemetery, was incorporated May 9th, 1867. It is designed for the use of the Roman Catholic Church. Accessible by Albany and Troy Horse cars and Rensselaer and Saratoga railroad.

NEW JERSEY STEAMBOAT COMPANY.

People's Evening Line

— FOR —

NEW YORK,

DAILY,

SUNDAYS EXCEPTED at 8 1-2 O'CLOCK P. M.

DEAN RICHMOND,

Capt. W. H. Christopher,

MONDAYS,
WEDNESDAYS
AND FRIDAYS,

DREW,

Capt. S. J. Roe,

TUESDAYS,
THURSDAYS
AND SATURDAYS,

At 8 1-2 o'clock P. M., or on arrival of Trains.

Hudson River R. R. Tickets Good for State Room Passage. These Boats will connect with the Trains of the N. Y. C. R. R., R. & S. R. R., and A. & S. R. R., due at Albany 8.15, 8.10 and 8.20 P. M.

All Checked Baggage transferred FREE, as usual.

An Agent of the Line at the Depot always on arrival of the Trains. Freight taken as cheap as by any other Line. For further particulars apply at the office.

Nos. 283 and 285 Broadway,

J. W. HARCOURT, Agent.

RAILROADS.

[On account of the numerous changes made in time tables at different seasons, we omit them. Such changes are usually advertised in the local papers.]

BOSTON AND ALBANY.—Station—Union Depot, Broadway, corner Colonie street. Six passenger trains leave here and five arrive daily.

HARLEM.—station—Union Depot, Broadway, corner Colonie street. Two passenger trains leave, via Boston and Albany, and two arrive daily.

N. Y. CENTRAL AND HUDSON RIVER.—Station—Union Depot, Broadway, corner Colonie street. Fourteen passenger trains leave and fourteen arrive daily.

RENSSELAER AND SARATOGA.—Station—Foot of Steuben street, Old Depot. Two passenger trains leave and three arrive daily.

SUSQUEHANNA.—Station—Broadway, fronting Steamboat Landing. Two passenger trains leave and two arrive daily.

TROY AND ALBANY.—Station—Foot of Steuben street and Union Depot. Nine passenger trains leave and nine arrive daily.

STEAMBOATS.

NEW YORK.

NEW JERSEY STEAMBOAT CO.—People's Line boats leave Steamboat Landing, foot of Madison avenue, every evening (Sundays excepted) at 8½ o'clock, or, on arrival of western trains.

TROY LINE.—Every evening, at 8½ o'clock, from Steamboat Landing.

DAY LINE.—Steamers stopping at intermediate landings, leave foot of Hamilton street every morning at 7 o'clock.

COXSACKIE.

Boats leave foot of Hamilton daily at 4 P. M., landing at Cedar Hill, Castleton, Coeymans, New Baltimore and Stuyvesant.

HUDSON AND CATSKILL.

Boats leave foot of Hamilton street daily at 3 P. M., landing at Cedar Hill, Castleton, Coeymans, New Baltimore, Stuyvesant and Coxsackie.

RONDOUT, PO'KEEPSIE AND NEWBURGH.

Boats leave foot of Hamilton street daily at 7½ o'clock A. M., stopping at intermediate landings.

J. V. B. CARTER,

(Successor to S. W. GIBBS,)

Pattern Maker,

AND DESIGNER.

Oriental and Modern Pattern Works,

No. 18 LIBERTY ST.,

ALBANY, N. Y.

PATTERNS OF ALL KINDS

Made at the Shortest Notice.

ALSO,

MODEL WORK,

WITH DISPATCH.

Turning and Scroll Sawing,

CARVING AND ORNAMENTING,

TO SUIT THE TIMES.

PRICES FOR HIRE OF HACKNEY COACHES.

The prices which may be charged by owners or drivers of hackney coaches, cabs, or other carriages, are as follows :

For conveying one passenger any distance within the paved streets	$0 50
For conveying one passenger over one mile, and not exceeding two miles	75
One passenger, over two miles, less than three	1 00
To Alms House and back, detaining hack one hour while there	1 00
For attending a funeral from any part of the city east of Robin street, to any public burying ground	2 00
For each passenger to Penitentiary and back, detaining hack thirty minutes while there	75

The owner or driver of every hackney coach, cab, or other carriage, shall be allowed for every hour the same may be detained, excepting as aforesaid, one dollar for the first hour, and for every additional hour, seventy-five cents; or the passenger or passengers may have the privilege of keeping the carriage all day, between the hours of eight in the morning and six in the evening, for five dollars; such owner or driver shall also be allowed to charge for every one hundred and twenty-eight pounds of baggage, at the same rate as for a passenger.

RATES OF CARTAGE.

SECTION 1. The price or rates which may be charged by cartmen for the carriage of articles in this city, including in such carriage, loading, carrying and unloading, shall be the following :

1st. When the distance does not exceed one mile—

For every hogshead of molasses, rum or other spirituous liquors, exceeding ninety gallons, fifty cents.

For every pipe of wine or spirituous liquor, fifty cents.

For every cask of molasses or spirituous liquors, exceeding thirty and less than sixty gallons, when carried singly, thirty cents.

For every hogshead of sugar, fifty cents.

For every tierce of sugar, twenty-five cents.

For removing every load of dirt or filth out of any of the streets, fifty cents.

For every load of household furniture, and housing the same, one dollar.

For every load of lumber, fifty cents.

For every load of flour, consisting of six barrels or more, thirty-seven cents.

For every single barrel of flour, twenty-five cents.

For every one hundred sides of sole leather, fifty cents.

For every one hundred green sides, seventy-five cents.

For every one hundred stoves, at the rate of eight dollars per hundred.

For every ton of iron, fifty cents.

For every three barrels of oil, thirty cents.

For every barrel over three, in the same load, six cents.

For every single trunk with carpet bag or bundle, twenty-five cents; two trunks or more, fifty cents.

For every load collected at two or more places, when delivered, fifty cents.

For every load not specified, thirty-seven cents.

2d. When the distance between the places of receiving and delivering exceeds a mile, one-half more than the above rates.

§ 2. If any cartman shall ask, demand, take, extort, or receive any greater rate or rates, price or prices for carting any goods, wares, merchandise or other things than hereinbefore mentioned and limited, or shall be guilty of embezzlement or deceit in the execution of his duty, or of cruelty to his horse, he shall be suspended from being a cartman by the Mayor, or in his absence, the Recorder; and such cartman shall, moreover, incur a penalty of five dollars for every such offence.

LODGES

AND

TEMPERANCE ORGANIZATIONS.

MASONIC.

F. and A. M., Regular Communications at Masonic Hall, 41 North Pearl street:

Mount Vernon Lodge, 3, 1st and 3d Mondays.
Masters' Lodge, 5, 2d and 4th Mondays.
Temple Lodge, 14, 1st and 3d Tuesdays.
Washington Lodge, 85, 2d and 4th Thursdays.
Wadsworth Lodge, 417, 2d and 4th Wednesdays.
Ancient City Lodge, 1st and 3d Wednesdays.
Temple Chapter, 5, 2d and 4th Tuesdays.
De Witt Clinton Council, R. and S. M., 22, 4th Friday.
Temple Commandery, 2, 1st and 3d Fridays.

CORNELIUS HILL,

Wholesale and Retail Dealer in

FRUITS, NUTS,

VEGETABLES,

Fish, Oysters and Clams,

NO. 48 BEAVER ST.,

ONE DOOR EAST OF PEARL,

ALBANY, N. Y.

ALSO, AGENT FOR

Shaker Garden Seeds.

ALL ORDERS PROMPTLY ATTENDED TO

AT THE SHORTEST NOTICE.

I. O. of O. F.
District Grand Committee of Albany, meet on the last Wednesday in January and on the third Wednesday in March (annual meeting) at Odd Fellows' Hall, Green street, corner of Beaver.

ENCAMPMENT.
New York Encampment 1, meet on the 1st and 3d Fridays of every month, at Odd Fellows' Hall.

DEGREE LODGES.
Albany City, 11, Tuesday evenings, Cooper's Building.
Excelsior, 15, 2d and 4th Friday evenings, Odd Fellows' Hall.

SUBORDINATE LODGES.
Hope 1, Monday evenings.
Clinton, 7, Wednesday evenings, Odd Fellows' Hall.
German Colonial, 16, Monday evenings, Commercial Building.
Fireman's, 19, Thursday evening, Odd Fellows' Hall.
American, 32, Tuesday evenings, Cooper's Building.
Mount Hermon, 38, Monday evenings, Cooper's Building.
Phœnix, 41, Tuesday evenings, Odd Fellows' Hall.
Mount Carmel, 76, Monday evenings, Commercial Building.
Samaritan, 93, Monday evenings, Odd Fellows' Hall.
Sch-Negh-Ta-Da, 87, Thursday evenings, Commercial Building.
Odd Fellows' Funeral Aid Association of the County of Albany, meet the second and fourth Fridays of each month, at Odd Fellows' Hall.

U. A. O. of D.
City Philanthropic Grove, 5, Friday evenings, Commercial Building.
Schiller Grove, 4, Thursday evenings, Commercial Building.
Union Supreme Arch Chapter, 4, first and third Sundays of each month, Commercial Building.

O. D. H. S.
Wm. Tell Lodge, 23, first and third Tuesdays of each month, 74 State street.

O. S. D. F.
Robert Blum Lodge, 38, first and third Fridays of each month, Commercial Building.

GRAND ARMY OF THE REPUBLIC.
Lew Benedict Post, 5, Friday evenings, Cooper's Building.
Post, 44, first and third Fridays of each month, 110 State street.

JOHN TAYLOR'S SON,

BREWER OF

DRAUGHT & BOTTLED ALES
And Porter.

DEPOTS:

133 Broadway, Albany,

334 GREENWICH ST.,

23 and 25 JAY STREET,

NEW YORK.

No. 117 Commercial Street, Boston.

TEMPLES OF HONOR.

Albany Social Temple, 22, Thursday evenings, 586 Broadway.
Excelsior Temple of Honor, 23, 110 State street.
Iturea Council, 3, 110 State street.
Star of Peace Social Temple, 4, 110 State street.
Tivoli Temple, 22, Tuesday evenings, 586 Broadway.

I. O. of G. S. AND D. of S.

Excelsior Union Lodge, 7, Friday evenings, Armory Building, Washington Parade Ground.
Graham Union Lodge, 16, Wednesday evenings, 74 State street.
Wesley Union Lodge, 4, Tuesday evenings, Lark corner Madison avenue.

I. O. Of G. T.

Albany City Lodge, Monday evenings, 110 State street.
Arbor Hill Union Lodge, Monday evenings, lecture room of the Arbor Hill M. E. Church.
Harrison Lodge, Tuesday evenings, 44 State street.

S. of T.

Albany Division, 24, Monday evenings, at 586 Broadway.
Band of Hope Mission, Sunday mornings, at 9 o'clock, Philip, corner of Hudson, D. L. Weaver, Superintendent.

BANKS.

Albany City National, 47 State street.
National Albany Exchange, 450 Broadway.
First National, 71 State street. Discount days, Mondays and Thursdays.
Hope Bank of Albany, State, corner James.
Mechanics' and Farmers' National, Broadway, corner Exchange.
Merchants' National of Albany, 458 Broadway.
National Commercial, 38 State street. Discount days, Wednesdays and Saturdays.
New York State National, 69 State. Discount day, Monday.
Union National of Albany, 446 Broadway.

SAVINGS BANKS.

Albany City, 47 State street.
Albany Exchange, 450 Broadway.
Albany, 38 State.
Mechanics' and Farmers', Broadway, corner Exchange.
National, 57 State street.

4

GEO. A. BIRCH & CO.,

WHOLESALE

GROCERS

AND DEALERS IN

Foreign and Domestic

LIQUORS,

477 and 479 Broadway,

AND

24 Dean Street,

ALBANY, N. Y.

TABLE OF DISTANCES, POPULATION, ETC.

The following table shows the distance from the place named to New York city, and the time at the same places when it is 12 o'clock, or mean noon, at New York, and the estimated population :

LOCALITIES.	Distance from New York, miles.	Time.	Estimated population, 1868.
		H. M.	
New York	....	12 00	1,000,000
Albany	146	11 58	80,000
Baltimore	185	11 50	220,000
Brooklyn	....	12 00	350,000
Boston	236	12 12	200,000
Buffalo	422	11 41	140,000
Charleston	797	11 36	45,000
Chicago	898	11 06	175,000
Cincinnati	662	11 19	200,000
Cleveland	581	11 30	60,000
Columbus	650	11 24	25,000
Detroit	663	11 24	75,000
Indianapolis............	825	11 14	35,000
Leavenworth	1,582	10 29	18,000
Louisville	934	11 14	75,000
Memphis	1,072	10 54	45,000
Mobile	1,448	11 05	40,000
New Orleans	1,597	10 56	175,000
Omaha	1,540	10 42	5,000
Philadelphia	87	11 56	570,000
Pittsburgh	481	11 36	55,000
Richmond	353	11 46	40,000
San Francisco..........	3,200	8 46	70,000
Savannah	890	11 31	25,000
St. Louis	1,087	10 55	175,000
Washington	225	11 48	....
Wheeling	565	11 33	....
Montreal	401	11 58	100,000
Liverpool	3,000	7 16 P. M.	450,000

.

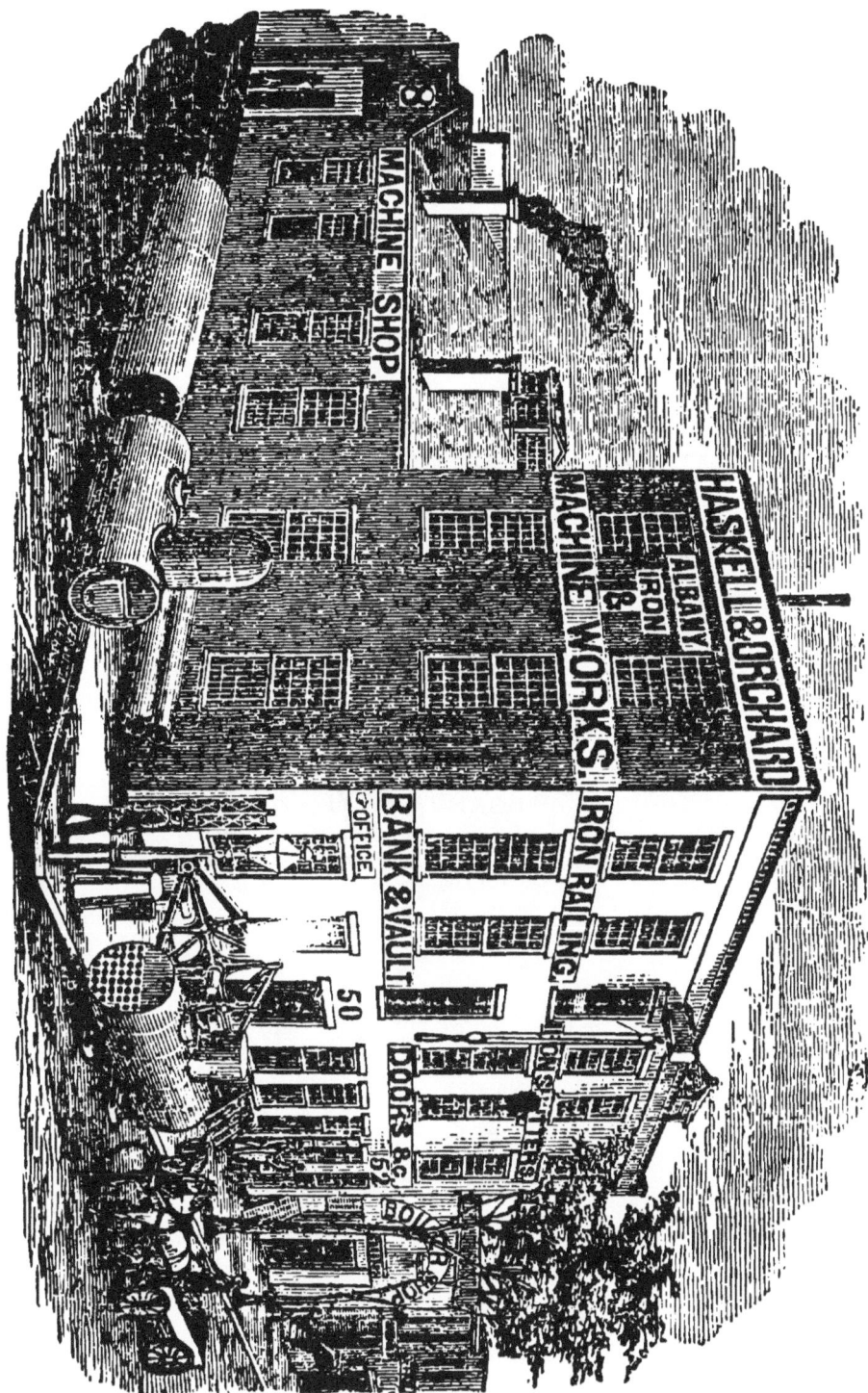

HASKELL & ORCHARD

ALBANY
IRON
&
MACHINE WORKS

MACHINE SHOP.

IRON RAILING.

BANK & VAULT

OFFICE

DOORS &C

50

52

NORMAN & TREADWELL,

ARCHITECTS

AND

CIVIL ENGINEERS,

51 NORTH PEARL STREET,

ALBANY, N. Y.

THOS. E. NORMAN.   E. PRENTICE TREADWELL.

ALBANY
STREET DIRECTORY.

The aim of the Street Directory is to give the location of each Street, and show what other Street or Place runs from or across it with the number at which they intersect. By its aid any person, even a stranger, can go to any numbered house without unnecessary travel.

From this List the location of any number on a Street can be easily ascertained. For instance, you wish to know at what part of Washington avenue 298 would come, you look for Washington avenue, and find that Knox crosses at 260 left, and Snipe at 310 left, so that 298 would be the sixth house from Snipe on the left hand side.

Albany & Schenectady Turnpike, from terminus of Central and Clinton aves. W.

Alexander, from 287 South Pearl W. to boundary.

Left.	Rt.	
10	11	Broad
22	21	Clinton
64	65	Elizabeth

Arch, from Quay W. to Grand.

Left.	Rt.	
10	9	Broadway
30	33	Church
48	49	Dallius
70	67	Green
96	99	Franklin
112	113	South Pearl
118	127	Broad
132		Clinton
146	145	Grand

Ash Grove Place, from 45 Broad W. to 114 Grand.

Bassett, from Quay W. to 286 South Pearl.

Left.	Rt.	
6	7	Broadway
16	15	Church
28	27	Dallius
56	53	Green
84	85	Franklin
96	101	South Pearl

Beaver, from 412 Broadway W. to 61 Eagle.

Left.	Rt.	
28	19	Green
48	49	South Pearl
58	57	William
66	....	Grand
	75	Lodge
	97	Wendell
110	....	Daniel
130	131	Eagle

Benjamin, from Whitehall road S. to boundary.

Bleecker, from Quay W. to
136 South Pearl.
Left. Rt.
6   7 Broadway
14   13 Church
28   23 Dallius
40   39 Green
75   74 Franklin
91   96 South Pearl
Bleecker Place, from junction Myrtle ave. and Philip
W. to 141 Eeagle.
Bradford, from Snipe W. to
boundary.
Left. Rt.
.... Robin
.... Perry
.... Quail
Broad, from 126 Madison
ave. S. to S. boundary.
Left. Rt.
40 .... Westerlo
.... Ash Grove Place.
94   99 Arch
144 145 Schuyler
180 175 Alexander
196 189 Nucella
Broadway, from S. to N.
boundaries.
Left. Rt.
2   1 Gansevoort
.... Vine
20   19 Nucella
.... Plumb
.... Bassett
.... 67 Cherry
.... Schuyler
.... Mulberry
.... Rensselaer
120 129 Arch
134 141 South Ferry
144 147 John
164 163 Westerlo
178 177 South Lansing
194 195 Herkimer
212 209 Bleecker
228 227 Madison avenue
.... 283 Hodge
286   Church

310   Pruyn
324 319 Hamilton
350 349 Division
361 Trotter's alley
392 391 Hudson
412   Beaver
430 427 State
441 Exchange
492 487 Maiden lane
554 551 Steuben
596 595 Columbia
638   Van Tromp
646 643 Orange
682   Clinton avenue
683 Quackenbush
719 Spencer
740   Wilson
786 777 Lumber
816 813 Colonie
834 .... Railroad avenue
823 North Lansing
841 De Witt
857 Lawrence
868   Van Woert
881 North Ferry
902   Kirk's alley
944 959 Thatcher
Canal, fr. 64 N. Pearl W. to
Snipe.
Left. Rt.
12   15 Chapel
40   Eagle
69 Cross
96   97 Hawk
154 155 Swan
.... Dove
.... Lark
.... Knox
.... Snipe
Capitol Place, from 61
Washington, S. to 211 State
Carroll, fr. 13 Spencer N. to
14 Lumber.
Catharine, fr. 21 Clinton W.
to Elizabeth
Centre, fr. 15 Lumber N. to
8 North Lansing
Left Rt.
.... Colonie

Mrs. CASTLE'S

EMPORIUM OF FASHIONS,

DRESS, CLOAK MAKING

And Pattern Establishment,

670 BROADWAY, ALBANY,

Between Orange and Clinton Ave.

Has always on hand the largest and most varied assortment of Styles of Patterns, trimmed in the most elegant, tasteful and fashionable manner, for Ladies' and Children's Dresses, and every kind of Garment.

Ladies, who wish to make their own Dresses, can have their measure taken and patterns cut in tissue paper, so that Dresses made after them are guaranteed to fit to perfection.

Mrs. CASTLE invites Dress-makers in want of reliable Patterns, either for Style or Sure Fitting, to patronize her establishment.

DRESS AND CLOAK MAKING

Done in the best finish and most elegant styles at short notice and moderate prices.

S. T. TAYLOR'S ADMIRABLE SYSTEM for Cutting Dresses, Basques, Gabrielles, &c., taught for $20, including system, Also,

Sole Agent for Mrs. Leake's Improved Diagram of 1870.

Mrs. CASTLE is satisfied she has two of the best methods of DRESS CUTTING, and invites the Ladies to call and test them. Satisfaction given or money refunded. A very superior Ladies' PAD constantly on hand.

MILLINERY IN ALL ITS BRANCHES DONE AT MRS. CASTLE'S,

670 BROADWAY.

.... North Lansing
Centre Alley, fr. Whitehall road S.
Central Ave., branches from Washington av. at Lark, N. W. to Albany and Schenectady turnpike.
Left Rt.
42 43 Knox
110 109 Snipe
176 .... Robin
232 229 Perry
.... 299 Quail
.... 349 Ontario
.... Partridge
.... Erie
.... Main avenue.
Chapel, fr. 20 Clinton ave. S. to 91 State.
Left Rt.
.... 15 Orange
14 17 Monroe
24 23 Canal
34 33 Columbia
42 37 Steuben
7 47 Pine
78 53 Maiden lane
86 67 State
Cherry, fr. Quay W. to 119 Franklin.
Left. Rt.
4 5 Broadway
30 29 Church
44 43 Dallius
64 65 Green
94 93 Franklin
Chestnut, fr. 78 Hawk W. to 65 Lark.
Left. Rt.
47 54 Swan
100 .... Dove
154 153 Lark.
Chestnut Alley, fr. 47 Hawk to Chestnut
Church, fr. 286 Broadway S. to Gansevoort
Left. Rt.
42 39 Madison avenue
56 53 Bleecker

64 67 Herkimer
82 77 South Lansing
92 87 Westerlo
102 97 John
108 107 South Ferry
122 121 Arch
134 133 Rensselaer
146 145 Mulberry
152 157 Schuyler
164 169 Cherry
178 181 Bassett
188 189 Plumb
.... Nucella
.... Vine
.... Gansevoort
Clinton, fr. 132 Arch S. to S. boundary.
Left. Rt.
9 Morton
21 Catharine
36 Schuyler
29 Delaware
60 41 Alexander.
72 59 Nucella
Clinton Avenue, fr. 682 Broadway W. to Albany & Schenectady turnpike.
Left. Rt.
10 17 North Pearl
12 Clinton square
20 Chapel
35 Ten Broeck
98 101 Hawk
156 155 Swan
210 211 Dove
.... Lark
.... Knox
.... Snipe
.... Robin
.... Perry
.... Quail
.... Ontario
.... Schenectady turnp.
Colonie, from Water W. to Lark.
Left. Rt.
.... Centre
.... Montgomery
.... 87 Broadway

Sash, Door and Blind Factory.

P. H. WEMPLE,

7 and 9 GRAND STREET,

Between Beaver & Hudson, **ALBANY, N. Y.**

Wholesale and Retail Dealer and Manufacturer of

Doors, Sash, Blinds, Shutters,

MOULDINGS, NEWELS,

Balusters, Stair Railings of any Style, &c.

A large assortment kept constantly on hand or made to order at short notice, at the lowest market prices.

☞ **ORDERS RESPECTFULLY SOLICITED.**

102 103 North Pearl
.... Ten Broeck
.... Swan
.... Lark
Columbia, fr. Quay W. to 1
  Eagle.
Left. Rt.
  14   15 Water
  24   25 Montgomery
  30   31 Broadway
  44   James
  58   57 North Pearl
  68   75 Chapel
  88   Lodge
 106 107 Eagle
Columbia Place, Eagle
  near Columbia.
Congress, fr. Capitol pl. W.
  to 161 Swan.
Cortland, fr. Del. turnpike
  W. to Alms house square.
Cross, from 69 Canal N. to
  100 Orange.
Left. Rt.
  .... 13 Monroe
  .... Orange
Dallius, from 46 Madison
  avenue S. to Gansevoort.
Left. Rt.
  6   7 Bleecker
  18   19 Herkimer
  30   31 South Lansing
  40   39 Westerlo
  50   49 John
  56   51 South Ferry
  68   67 Arch
  76   75 Rensselaer
  88   87 Mulberry
  98   99 Schuyler
 108 111 Cherry
 120 123 Bassett
 130 131 Plumb
 .... Nucella
 .... Vine
 ....:. Gansevoort
Daniel, from 110 Beaver S.
  W. to 129 Eagle.
Day, from Whitehall road to
  turnpike.

Dean, from 14 Maiden lane
  S. to 13 Hudson
Left. Rt.
  39   42 Exchange
  47   48 State
  61   60 Hudson
Delaware, from 29 Clinton
  W. to Dove
Left Rt.
  48   47 Elizabeth
 .... Eagle
 .... Hawk
 .... Swan
 .... Dove
Delaware Turnpike, from
  Madison ave. opp. Lark S.
De Witt, from Montgomery
  W. to 841 Broadway.
Division, from 71 Quay W.
  to 72 South Pearl.
Left. Rt.
  6   7 Broadway
  24   25 Liberty
  34   35 Union
  48   49 Green
  80   South Pearl
Dove, from Clinton avenue
  S. to S. boundaries.
Left. Rt.
 .... Orange
 .... Canal
 .... Spruce
 .... Elk
 .... 11 Washington ave.
 .... 21 Spring
  30   31 State
  40   41 Chestnut
  48   53 Lancaster
  60   57 Jay
  68   67 Hudson
 .... Hamilton
 106 109 Madison avenue
 116 115 Jefferson
 120 121 Elm
 .... Park avenue
 .... Warren
 .... Morton
Droogan Alley, from 1
  Clinton W.

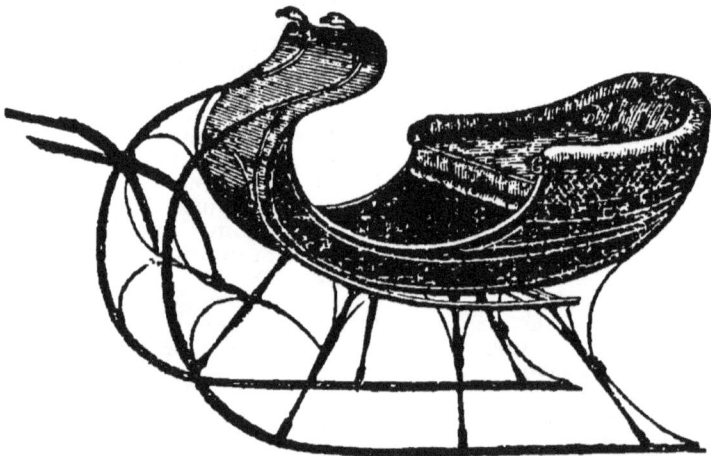

Left.	Rt.	

Eagle, from 40 Canal S. to S. boundary.

Left. Rt.

		Spruce
....		Columbia
		Elk
....		Steuben
....		Pine -
		Washington avenue
....		Maiden lane
....	....	State
31		Howard
	46	Lancaster
61		Beaver
	66	Jay
75	76	Hudson
89		Plain
93	92	Hamilton
	104	Wendell alley
109	114	Madison avenue
121		Madison place
	122	Jefferson
129	132	Elm
141		Bleecker place
155	154	Myrtle avenue
165	164	Johnson alley
175	174	Park avenue.
....	....	Warren
....	....	Morton

Eagle Alley, from opposite 19 Hamilton S. to opposite 4 Pruyn

Elizabeth, from Warren S. to S. boundary.

Left. Rt.

....	....	Morton
....	....	Catharine
....	....	Delaware
....	....	Alexander
....	....	Nucella

Elk, from Eagle W. to Dove

Left. Rt.

26	25	Hawk
....	....	Swan
....	....	Dove

Elm, from 75 Grand W. to Delaware turnpike

Left. Rt.

| 34 | 35 | Philip |

68	67	Eagle
120	121	Hawk
172	173	Swan
228	229	Dove
270	271	Delaware turnpike

Erie, from S. boundary N. to Schenectady turnpike

Left. Rt.

....	....	Myrtle avenue .
....	....	Madison avenue
....	....	Western avenue
....	....	Hudson
....	....	Lancaster
....	....	State
....	....	Spring
....	....	Washington avenue
....	....	Schenectady turnp.

Exchange, from 47 Quay W. to 441 Broadway

Left. Rt.

| 12 | 9 | Dean |
| 18 | 19 | Broadway |

Fayette, from 1 Park Place W. to 143 Swan

Left. Rt.

| 16 | 17 | Hawk |
| 80 | 79 | Swan |

First, fr. 22 Ten Broeck W. to W. boundary.

Left. Rt.

40	....	Hawk
82	79	Swan
....	....	Dove
....	....	Lark
....	....	Knox
....	....	Snipe
....	....	Robin

Foundry Place, fr. 56 N. Ferry S

Franklin, fr. 94 Madison ave. S. to 25 Gansevoort

Left. Rt.

....	2	Bleecker
7	4	Herkimer
29	28	Westerlo
39	....	John
51	50	South Ferry
67	68	Arch
81	80	Rensselaer

93	....	Mulberry
107	106	Schuyler
119	....	Cherry
131	130	Bassett
....	....	Plumb
157	162	Nucella
169	....	Vine
179	178	Gansevoort

Fulton, fr. 8 Plain S. to 125 Madison avenue

Left. Rt.
12	13	Hamilton
....	25	Van Zandt
30	33	Madison avenue

Gansevoort, fr. 1 Broadway W. to 334 South Pearl

Left. Rt.
....	....	Church
....	....	Dallius
2	1	Green
24	25	Franklin
40	41	South Pearl

Garden, fr. 101 Dove W. to Lark

Grand, from 66 Beaver S. to 15 Morton

Left. Rt.
	11	Grand alley
18	17	Hudson
28	25	Plain
44	43	Hamilton
54	55	Van Zandt
66	65	Madison avenue
	75	Elm
	93	Wilbur
114		Ash Grove place.
	125	Myrtle avenue
	139	Johnson alley
	149	Park avenue
....		Arch
	157	Warren
168	169	Morton

Grand Alley, fr. 11 Grand W

Green, fr. 50 State S. to 2 Gansevoort

Left Rt.
	7	Norton
24	19	Beaver

46	41	Hudson
58	55	Division
74	69	Hamilton
100	99	Madison avenue
104	101	Bleecker
114	111	Herkimer
126	121	South Lansing
138	131	Westerlo
142	143	John
148	151	South Ferry
174	167	Arch
180	181	Rensselaer
192	....	Mulberry
204	205	Schuyler
208	217	Cherry
218	229	Bassett
232	233	Plumb
244	247	Nucella
258	259	Vine
278	283	Gansevoort

Hall Place, fr. Ten Broeck, between Second and Third

Hamilton, fr. 79 Quay W. to 125 Lark

Left Rt.
6	7	Broadway
....		Eagle alley
24	25	Liberty
38	39	Union
56	55	Green
72	....	Rose
94	95	South Pearl
100	103	Fulton
112	115	Grand
140	147	Philip
162	171	Eagle
202	199	High
222	219	Hawk
....	239	Hamilton place
272	271	Swan
316	323	Dove
370	373	Lark

Hamilton Place, from 239 Hamilton N

Hawk, fr. S. boundary N. to 40 First

Left Rt.
....	....	Morton
....	....	Warren

H. TUNNY,

MERCHANT

TAILOR,

— AND —

CLOTHIER,

679 Broadway,

ALBANY, N. Y.

∞

A LARGE ASSORTMENT OF

FRENCH & ENGLISH CLOTHS AND CASSIMERES

Constantly on hand and adapted to

The Finest Trade with the Lowest Prices.

....	....	Park avenue
....	....	Myrtle avenue
4	5	Elm
10	11	Jefferson
18	19	Madison avenue
36	33	Hamilton
42		Watson avenue
44	45	Hudson
48	47	Jay
62	63	Lancaster
78		Chestnut
90	89	State
104	101	Washington av
106	105	Fayette
114	115	Elk
....	....	Spruce
....	....	Canal
....	....	Orange
....	....	Clinton avenue
178	177	First

Herkimer, fr. 104 Quay W. to 142 South Pearl

Left. Rt.

8	9	Broadway
16	17	Church
38	39	Dallius
50	51	Green
80	89	Franklin
103	109	South Pearl

High, from 108 State S. to 239 Madison avenue

Left. Rt.

26	25	Lancaster
28	27	Jay
40	41	Hudson
54	51	Hamilton
54½		Wendell Alley
60	61	Madison avenue

Hodge, from 95 Quay W. to 283 Broadway

Howard, from 13 S. Pearl W. to Eagle

Left. Rt.

22	....	William
36	35	Lodge
52		Wendell
70	69	Eagle

Hudson, from 57 Quay W. to W. boundary

Left. Rt.

....	13	Dean
24	17	Broadway
36		Liberty
42		Union
56	53	Green
82	75	South Pearl
....	87	William
98	95	Grand
110	....	Philip
	129	Daniel
132	131	Eagle
156	157	High
174	177	Hawk
230	231	Swan
298	291	Dove
358	353	Lark
380	385	Willett
....	....	Knox

Hunter's Alley, from 71 Swan W

Jackson, from 47 Spencer N. to Lumber

James, from 63 State N. to 44 Columbia

Left. Rt.

20	19	Maiden lane
48	49	Steuben
60	55	Columbia

Jay, from 66 Eagle W. to 89 Lark

Left. Rt.

32	31	High
52	51	Hawk
....	....	Swan
166	161	Dove
220	223	Lark

Jefferson, from 124 Eagle W. to Delaware turnpike

Left. Rt.

60	57	Hawk
122	121	Swan
180	179	Dove
234	233	Delaware turnpike

John, from 130 Quay W. to 39 Franklin

Great Western

MUTUAL LIFE INSURANCE COMPANY
OF NEW YORK.

J. A. FREMIRE, Agt., 444 Broadway,
ALBANY, N. Y.

We would advise our friends and the public, and all those who anticipate and desire to insure in a good and reliable Company, to give the Agent of the Great Western a call before they invest their money elsewhere. We will vouch for all we say to the public. They will find many advantages in

THE GREAT WESTERN MUTUAL LIFE INSURANCE CO.

that no other Company gives to the insured. First, it is a purely Mutual Company; the entire surplus over the actual cost of insurance being divided equally among the assured. The stockholders receive only seven per cent., while in most every other Company the stockholders receive out of the funds that belong to the insured, over legal interest, from twenty to thirty per cent. This amount is put into the pockets to enrich the stockholders before dividends are paid to the policy holder. The Great Western issues all approved and every desirable form of policies, and all payments and dividends are non-forfeitable, and dividends are declared annually, and are paid in cash. No conditions whatever are imposed upon the insured in respect to residence or travel in any part of the civilized world, and no restrictions in regard to occupation are excepted as requiring the special permit from the Company, or the payment of an extra premium; and the insured are allowed thirty days grace for the payment of premiums. One annual payment continues a policy in force two years, and five payments over ten years; and if the death of the party occur within that time, the Company are bound by their charter to pay the amount of the policy the same as if there had been no elapse of premium. The above mentioned features, embracing every accommodation with entire security to the Company, make

The Great Western Mutual one of the most Liberal Life Insurance Companies in the United States.

The facilities which it affords the uninsured are such as leave him no excuse for neglecting his duty to himself and family. Nothing but the actual gift of a policy can exceed the advantages offered by this Company.

Left. Rt.
.... Broadway
0   10 Church
19 20 Dallius
35 36 Green
63 64 Franklin
Johnson's Alley, from 139
Grand W. to Hawk
Left. Rt.
.... Philip
.... Eagle
.... Hawk
King's Place, from 119 N.
Swan
Kirk's Alley, from 902
Broadway W. to 305 North
Pearl
Knox, from 288 Lumber S.
to S. boundary
Left. Rt.
.... Third
.... Second
.... First
.... Clinton avenue
.... Canal
.,.. .... Spruce
.... Elk
.... Sherman
.... Central avenue
.... Western avenue
.... Washington ave
.... Spring
.... State
.... Lancaster
.... Hudson
.... Hamilton
.... Madison avenue
.... Yates
.... Morris
.... Myrtle avenue
Lancaster, from 46 Eagle
W. to W. boundary
Left. Rt.
.... 11 Park
28   29 High
48   49 Hawk
102 99 Swan
150 153 Dove
202 205 Lark

.... Willett
.... Knox
Lancaster Alley, from 3
Lancaster N. W. to 2 Park
Lark, from Colonie S. to S.
boundary
Left. Rt.
.... Lumber
20 21 Third
28 39 Second
.... First
.... Clinton avenue
.... Orange
.... Canal
.... Spruce
.... Elk
.... 14 Sherman
27 26 Washington ave
53 58 Spring
63 68 State
65 .... Chestnut
77 76 Lancaster
89 .... Jay
105 108 Hudson
125 .... Hamilton
145 148 Madison avenue
Lawrence, from the river
W. to 855 Broadway
Left. Rt.
.... Water
22 21 Montgomery
88 89 Broadway
Lawrence Court, from 55
Lawrence N.
Learned, from 20 N. Ferry
N. to Thacher
Liberty, from 36 Hudson S.
to 39 Madison avenue
Left. Rt.
16 15 Divison
28 29 Hamilton
36 .... Pruyn
68 71 Madison avenue
Little Basin, from Water
between N. Lansing and
Lawrence
Lodge, from 88 Columbia S.
to 75 Beaver

MANUFACTURE

Ladies' and Gents'

Paper Collars, &c.

ALBANY
PAPER COLLAR COMPANY,

WAREROOMS:

No. 619, 621, 623 and 625 BROADWAY.

Manufactory, Montgomery Street.

All Styles of LADIES' and GENTS'

PAPER COLLARS and CUFFS.

New Styles Frequently Advanced.

Ed. Elisha Mack, {MACK & CO.} Stephen Jarvis,

General Managers.

Left.	Rt.	
8	7	Steuben
14	15	Pine
28	29	Maiden lane
36	37	State
48	45	Howard
66	65	Beaver

Lumber District, from head North Ferry N.

Lumber, from Water W. to W. boundary

Left.	Rt.	
14	....	Carroll
....	15	Center •
....	....	Montgomery
....	....	Jackson
64	65	Broadway
86	87	North Pearl
106	103	Ten Broeck
146	147	Swan
246	249	Lark
288	293	Knox
....	....	Snipe
....	....	Robin

Madison avenue, from Quay at Steamboat Landing W. to W. boundary

Left.	Rt.	
12	....	Broadway
26	21	Church
	39	Liberty
46		Dallius
	47	Union
68	65	Green
	85	Rose
94		Franklin
108	109	South Pearl
	125	Fulton
126	....	Broad
142	143	Grand
180	177	Philip
....	207	Eagle
	239	High
266	263	Hawk
324	323	Swan
374	379	Dove
422	423	Lark
....	....	Delaware turnpike
....	477	Willett

		Knox
....	....	Snipe
....	....	Robin
....	....	Perry
....	....	Quail
....	....	Ontario
....	....	Partridge
....	....	Erie
....	....	Main

Madison Place, fr. Philip W. to 123 Eagle S. side of Madison avenue

Maiden Lane, from 35 Quay W. to Eagle

Left.	Rt.	
14	....	Dean
26	25	Broadway
30	29	James
40	41	North Pearl
52	49	Chapel
60	63	Lodge
88	89	Eagle ^

Mercer, . from Delaware turnpike to Alms House sq.

Merchant's Place, from 162 Hamilton S.

Monroe, from 84 N. Pearl W. to op. 14 Cross

Left.	Rt.	
12	11	Chapel
58	59	Cross

Montgomery, from Steuben N. to Lawrence

Left.	Rt.	
24	25	Columbia
36	37	Orange
64	59	Quackenbush
82	....	Spencer
....	....	Lumber
....	....	Colonie
....	....	North Lansing
....	....	De Witt
....	....	Lawrence

Morris, from Delaware sq. to N. boundary

Morton, from 9 Clinton W. to Delaware turnpike · .

Left.	Rt.	
	15	Grand

44	35	Elizabeth	58	63	Columbia
66	67	Eagle	66		Canal
....	....	Swan		83	Van Tromp
....	....	Delaware turnpike	84	....	Monroe

Mulberry, from Quay W. to 93 Franklin

Left. Rt.

....	....	Broadway	94	95	Orange
14	19	Church	....	107	Clinton avenue
26	25	Dallius	142	143	Wilson
38	41	Green	182	193	Lumber
60	75	Franklin	216	217	Colonie
			280	275	Railroad avenue
			272	275	Van Woert
				305	Kirk's alley
			342	343	Thacher

Myrtle Avenue, from 123 Grand W. to W. boundary

Left. Rt.

24	23	Philip
52	55	Eagle
74	75	Hawk
96	....	Swan
:...	....	Dove
....	....	Lark
....	....	Knox
....	....	Snipe
....	....	Robin
....	....	Perry
.*..	....	Quail
....	....	Ontario
..:.	....	Partridge
....	....	Eric
....	....	Main

North Ferry, from the River W. to 881 Broadway

Left. Rt.

....	....	Water
....	....	Montgomery
....	....	Rathbone
....	59	Learned
98	99	Broadway

North Lansing, fr. Water W. to 823 Broadway

Left. Rt.

8	....	Center
26	27	Montgomery
80	81	Broadway

North Pearl, from 77 State N. to Thacher

Left. Rt.

14	25	Maiden lane
46	51	Steuben

Norton, from 7 Green W. to 24 S. Pearl

Nucella, from Quay W. to W. boundary

Left. Rt.

....	....	Broadway
....	....	Church
....	....	Dallius
58	61	Green
78	79	Franklin
	95	Onet's alley
96	97	South Pearl
108	107	Broad
118	117	Clinton
....	....	Elizabeth
....	....	Eagle

Odell, from Van Vechten S.

Onet's Alley, from 95 Nucella N.

Ontario, from South to N. boundaries

....	....	Second
....	....	Clinton avenue
....	....	Elk
....	....	Sherman
....	....	Central avenue
....	....	Washington avenue
....	....	State
....	....	Lancaster
....	....	Western avenue
....	....	Hudson
....	....	Yates
....	....	Morris
....	....	Madison avenue
....	....	Myrtle avenue

Oak, W. of Knox, Arbor Hill
Orange, from Quay W. to Dove

Left. Rt.
2   1   Water
18   15   Montgomery
30   25   Broadway
50   37   N. Pearl
.... Clinton place
56   55   Chapel
104 .... Cross
132   135   Hawk
194   189   Swan
226   227   Dove

Osborn, from Elizabeth S. to Bethlehem line
Park, from 154 State S. to 11 Lancaster
Park Avenue, from 149 Grand West to Delaware turnpike

Left. Rt.
36   37   Philip
76   75   Eagle
.... Swan
.... Dove
.... Delaware turnpike

Park Place, rear of Capitol and Academy Parks
Partridge, fr S. boundary N. to Central avenue
.... Myrtle avenue
.... Madison avenue
.... Western avenue
.... State
.... Washington avenue
.... Schenectady turnp.

Perry, from Alms House sq. N. to N. boundary

Left. Rt.
.... Myrtle avenue
.... Morris
.... Yates
.... Madison avenue
.... Hudson
.... Western avenue
.... Lancaster
.... State

.... Spring
.... Washington avenue
.... Central avenue
.... Sherman
.... Clinton avenue

Pier, from the foot of Lawrence S. to the foot of Hamilton
Phœnix Place, from 114 Hudson S.
Pine, from Eagle E. to 7 Chapel

Left. Rt.
8   9   Lodge
18   19   Chapel

Philip, from 114 Hudson S. to Morton

Left. Rt.
....   17   Plain
26   23   Hamilton
44   ....   Van Zandt
54   49   Madison avenue
58   59   Elm
76   Wilbur
....   91   Bleecker place
98   97   Myrtle avenue
108   105   Johnson alley
118   115   Park avenue
.... Warren
.... Morton

Plain, from 51 S. Pearl W. to 89 Eagle

Left Rt.
8   Fulton
18   19   Grand
38   31   Philip
.... Eagle

Pleasant, from Madison av. N. to Schenectady turnpike
Plumb, from Quay W. to op. 146 Franklin

Left. Rt.
.... Broadway
6   5   Church
16   17   Dallius
.... Green
.... Franklin

Providence, from Delaware turnpike N. to Schenectady turnpike
Pruyn, from 310 Broadway W. to 36 Liberty
Left. Rt.
2   1   Broadway
    3   Eagle
10   11   Liberty
Quackenbush, from Quay W. to 685 Broadway
Left. Rt.
....   Water
14   13   Montgomery
24   29   Broadway
Quail, from N. to S. boundaries
Left. Rt.
....   Myrtle avenue
....   Madison avenue
....   Hudson
....   Western avenue
....   State
....   Washington avenue
....   Bradford
....   Central avenue
.... Sherman
....   Elk
....   Clinton avenue
Quay, along the river from 2 Quackenbush S. to South boundary
Left. Rt.
....   Orange
....   Columbia
35   Maiden lane
47   Exchange
52   State
57   Hudson
71   Division
79   Hamilton
95   Hodge
96   Madison avenue
100   Bleecker
108   Herkimer
114   South Lansing
125   Westerlo
130   John
....   Arch

.... Rensselaer
.... Mulberry
.... Cherry
.... Bassett
.... Plumb
.... Nucella
.... Vine
.... Gansevoort
Railroad Avenue, from Lumber N. W. to 19 Van Woert
Left. Rt.
....   Lumber
....   Broadway
....   Van Woert
Rathbone, from N. Ferry N. to Thacher
Rensselaer, from Quay W. to 232 S. Pearl
Left. Rt.
....   Broadway
12   13   Church
28   27   Dallius
42   43   Green
66   65   Franklin
84   81   South Pearl
Road, from 144 Canal S. W. to Swan
Robin, from S. to N. boundaries
Left. Rt.
....   Myrtle avenue
....   Morris
....   Yates
....   Madison ave
....   Hudson
....   State
....   Washington avenue
....   Bradford
....   Central avenue
....   Sherman
....   Elk
....   Clinton avenue
....   First
....   Second
....   Third
....   Lumber
....   Colonie

TAYLOR, HAMLIN & CO.,

Importers and Manufacturers of

Coach & Saddlery

HARDWARE,

420 BROADWAY, 420
ALBANY, N.Y.

JOHN RHODES,

THREE-SPRING

BUSINESS WAGON

And Sleigh Manufacturer,

No. 73 Herkimer Street,

Residence 134 Madison Ave., ALBANY, N.Y.

Business Wagons and Sleighs always on hand, or made to order at short notice, and at the very lowest prices.

Rose, from 72 Hamilton S.
   85 Madison avenue
Left. Rt.
     15 Rose Street alley
  20 19 Madison avenue
Rose Street Al., from 19
  Rose N.
Schuyler, from Broadway
  W. to 36 Clinton
Left. Rt.
  20 21 Church
  28 27 Dallius
  46 45 Green
  78 81 Franklin
  92 93 South Pearl
  98 99 Broad
 110 109 Clinton
Second, fr opposite 47 Ten
  Broeck W. to W. boundary
Left. Rt.
      Hall place
  54 55 Swan
 158 159 Lark
      Knox
      Snipe
      Robin
Sherman, from 14 Lark W.
  to W. boundary
Left. Rt.
      Knox
      Snipe
      Robin
      Perry
      Quail
      Ontario
      Partridge
Snipe, fr. S. to N. boundary
Left. Rt.
      Myrtle avenue
      Morris
      Yates
      Madison avenue
      Hamilton
      Hudson
      Lancaster
      State
      Washington avenue
      Central avenue
      Sherman

      Elk
      Clinton avenue
      First
      Second
      Third
      Lumber
      Colonie.
South Ferry, fr. 134 Broadway W. to 208 S. Pearl
Left. Rt.
  10 11 Church
  28 27 Dallius
  44 41 Green
  70 71 Franklin
  84 83 South Pearl
South Lansing, from Quay
  W. to 21 Franklin
Left. Rt.
      Broadway
   8   7 Church
  22 23 Dallius
  42 43 Green
  72 71 Franklin
South Pearl, from 88 State
  S. to S. boundary
Left. Rt.
    13 Howard
  24   Norton
  34 19 Beaver
  62 43 Hudson
     57 Plain
  82   Division
  81 104 Hamilton
     93 Van Zandt
 136 137 Madison avenue
 136   Bleecker
 144   Herkimer
 172 149 Westerlo
 208   South Ferry
 228 205 Arch
 242   Rensselaer
 274 249 Schuyler
 298   Bassett
    287 Alexander
 326 305 Nucella
 344   Gansevoort
      Whitehall road
Spencer, from Water W. to
  719 Broadway

TURKISH

ELECTRO-CHEMICAL AND

Sulphurous Vapor Baths

696 Broadway, Albany, N.Y.

(One Square North of Delavan House.)

Horse Cars to and from all parts of the city pass the doors of this house.

HOURS FOR BATHING.

From 7 A. M. to 9 P. M., and Sundays from 7 A. M. to 12 M. Separate apartments for Ladies, and the utmost privacy is observed.

Single Ticket..................$1.25 | Twelve Tickets..............$10.00
Five Tickets.................... 5.00 | Simple Hot or Cold Bath,   30

MODUS OPERANDI OF THE TURKISH BATH.

The Bather enters the Reception Room, registers his name, and is there shown into a Dressing Room, where he disrobes, each bather having a separate apartment. A sheet is then provided for him, and he is now ready for the "Tepidarium," or warm room. There his head is wet with cold water, also drinks freely of water, and reclines or sits on a resting chair for ten or fifteen minutes, until the skin becomes soft and moist. He is then ready for the "Calidarium," or hot room, until profuse perspiration takes place, the head meanwhile being kept wet with *cold water*. He is then taken out and shampooed by the attendant on a couch where he is manipulated, not a muscle escaping the shampooer's hands. That process completed, he is shampooed from head to foot with perfumed Glycerine Soap, which leaves the skin "soft as velvet." Then comes the Spray Bath, warm at first, then cool, then cold; and so gradual is the change of temperature that no shock is given to the system. When the bather is sufficiently cooled, a hot dry sheet is thrown over him, he is ushered into the "Frigidarium," or cooling room. Here, reclining or sitting, he remains until thoroughly cool and dry, when he is ready to dress, a wiser, cleaner and happier man.

THE LADIES GO THROUGH THE SAME ROUTINE.

Non-bathers often express an alarm lest the Bath may be weakening. But the Bath strengthens, it never weakens. The idea of weakening is suggested by the loss of fluids by perspiration; but this loss is a gain, and not a loss. The expulsion of watery fluids from the economy is a natural process, necessary to our very existence, and affects the nervous and muscular powers of the individual beneficially.

R. L. MARTIN, Manager.

Left.	Rt.	
2	1	Water
12	13	Carroll
30	31	Montgomery
46	47	Jackson
60	61	Broadway

Spring, from 21 Dove W. to Knox

Left.	Rt.	
2	1	Dove
136	131	Lark
....	....	Knox

Spruce, from 3 Columbia place W.

Left.	Rt.	
....	....	Hawk
....	....	Swan
....	....	Dove
....	....	Lark

State, from 52 Quay W. to 1 Western avenue

Left.	Rt.	
16	17	Dean
82	29	Broadway
50		Green
	63	James
88		S. Pearl
	77	N. Pearl
	87	Chapel
116	99	Lodge
144	125	Eagle
154		Park
168		High
184	....	Hawk
	211	Capitol place
234	241	Swan
294	293	Dove
316	347	Lark
362		Willett
402	403	Knox
....	....	Snipe
....	....	Robin
....	....	Western avenue

Steamboat Landing, Quay between Hodge and Madison avenue

Steuben, from Montgomery W. to Eagle

Left.	Rt.	
....	....	Broadway
14	15	James
26	29	N. Pearl
36	35	Chapel
44	43	Lodge
60	61	Eagle

Swan, from N. to S. boundaries

Left.	Rt.	
....	....	Colonie
17	20	Lumber
41	49	Third
61	62	Second
79	84	First
....	....	Clinton avenue
....	....	Orange
....	....	Canal
....	....	Road
....	....	Spruce
139	138	Elk
143		Fayette
147	158	Washington avenue
161		Congress
171	172	State
....	....	Chestnut
156	155	Lancaster
160	161	Jay
181	180	Hudson
191		Washington avenue
195	196	Hamilton
209	210	Madison avenue
219	214	Jefferson
225	224	Elm
....	....	Myrtle avenue
....	....	Park avenue
....	....	Warren
....	....	Morton

Ten Broeck, fr. 35 ave. N. W. to Colonie

Left.	Rt.	
22	....	First
....	33	Wilson
....	....	Second
....	....	Third
....	....	Lumber
....	....	Colonie

Thacher, fr. the Erie canal W. to 343 North Pearl

CHARLES FERGUSON,

Manufacturer of and Dealer in all kinds of

CABINET

FURNITURE!

USES NOTHING BUT

THOROUGH-SEASONED LUMBER,

And by the assistance of the most improved Machinery is enabled to sell a first-class article at as LOW a price, if not lower, than the same class of goods can be bought for either in Boston or New York.

Office and Warerooms,

549 BROADWAY,

ALBANY, N. Y.

☞ Manufactory, 7 and 9 Pruyn Street.

Left.	Rt.	
...	...	Water
...	...	Montgomery
...	...	Learned
...	...	Rathbone
...	...	Broadway
...	...	North Pearl

Third, fr. op. 79 Ten Broeck W. to boundary

Left.	Rt.	
48	49	Swan
158	159	Lark
...	315	Knox
...	...	Snipe
...	...	Robin

Tivoli, (formerly Tivoli Hollow) from Troy road to N. boundary

Trotter's Alley, from Quay W. to 361 Broadway

Union, from 42 Hudson S. to 47 Madison avenue

Left.	Rt.	
12	11	Division
24	25	Hamilton
66	61	Madison avenue

Van Tromp, fr. 638 Broadway W. to 83 N. Pearl

Van Woert, fr. 868 Broadway W.

Left.	Rt.	
18	19	Railroad avenue
20	...	North Pearl

Van Zandt, from 87 S. Pearl W. to 44 Philip

Left	Rt.	
...	...	Fulton
24	25	Grand
52	51	Philip

Vine, from Quay W. to 169 Franklin

Left.	Rt.	
...	...	Broadway
...	...	Church
...	...	Dallius
...	...	Green
...	...	Franklin

Warren, from 157 Grand W. to Alms House

Left.	Rt.	
...	...	Elizabeth
...	...	Philip
...	...	Eagle
...	...	Hawk
...	...	Swan
...	...	Dove
...	...	Delaware turnpike

Warren Street Alley, from Warren street S. W. to Elizabeth

Washington Avenue, fr. Eagle op. City Hall, W. to W. boundary

Left.	Rt.	
2	1	Park place
....	29	Hawk
64	....	Capitol place
90	91	Swan
150	145	Dove
200	199	Lark
260	....	Knox
310	325	Snipe
...	...	Robin
...	...	Perry
...	...	Quail
...	...	Ontario
...	...	Partridge
...	...	Erie
...	...	Main avenue

Washington Sq., State and Madison avenue between Willett and Knox

Water, from 15 Columbia N. to 1 N. Ferry

Left.	Rt.	
46	...	Orange
70	...	Quackenbush
...	...	Spencer
112	109	Lumber
126	...	Colonie
...	...	North Lansing
...	...	Lawrence
...	...	North Ferry

Watson's Avenue, from 42 Hawk W. to 191 Swan

Wendell, from 97 Beaver N. to 52 Howard

WM. P. HALPEN,

WHOLESALE DEALER IN

WHITE SAND,

COAL OF ALL SIZES,

☞ Also, OILS OF ALL DESCRIPTIONS. ☜

OFFICE:

205 & 207 Broadway,

SOUTH OF STEAMBOAT LANDING,

ALBANY, N. Y.

WOODEN WARE, &c.

J. & J. DORAN,

DEALERS IN

Tubs, Pails, Washboards, Mop Handles, Butter Bowls,
Churns, Measures, Clothes' Washers and Wringers,
Brooms, Brushes, Bed Cords, Coil Rope, Mats,
Twine ; Market, Clothes and Corn
Baskets ; Flour Sieves, Bird
Cages, Step Ladders,
Childrens' Chairs, Clothes' Frames, Water Filters & Coolers,
CHILDREN'S CARRIAGES, REFRIGERATORS, &c.

393 BROADWAY Corner of HUDSON STREET.

Wendell's Alley, from 104 Eagle W. to 54 High

West, from Robin W. to Quail

Left. Rt.

.... Perry

.... Quail

Westerlo, from 125 Quay W. to 40 Broad

Left. Rt.

5 .... Broadway
13   12 Church
29   30 Dallius
41   42 Green
67   66 Franklin
79   78 South Pearl
95   86 Broad

Western Ave., branches from 325 Washington ave., and Snipe W. to W. boundary

Left. Rt.

.... Perry
.... Quail
.... Ontario
.... Partridge
.... Erie
.... Main

Whitehall Road, fr. Bethleham N. W.

Wilbur, from 93 Grand W. to 76 Philip

Willett, from 362 State S. to 447 Madison avenue

Left. Rt.

41 .... Lancaster
68 .... Hudson
112 ...; Madison avenue

William, from 22 Howard S. to 87 Hudson

Left. Rt.

.... 12 Beaver
33   34 Hudson

Wilson, from 740 Broadway W. to 33 Ten Broeck

Left. Rt.

11   15 North Pearl
32   27 Ten Broeck

Yates, from Delaware sq. W. to W. boundary

Left. Rt.

.... Lark
.... Knox
.... Snipe
.... Robin

L. J. LLOYD,

SADDLE, HARNESS,

TRUNK, VALISE & CARPET BAG

MANUFACTURER,

Engine, Hose & Military Equipments

MADE TO ORDER,

AND

Everything Pertaining to the Business.

340 and 342 BROADWAY,

ALBANY, N. Y.

AMUSEMENTS.

ACADEMY OF MUSIC, Division, between South Pearl and Green streets.
TRIMBLE OPERA HOUSE, South Pearl, between Beaver and Hudson streets.
NATIONAL THEATRE, South Pearl, between Alexander and Nucella streets.

HALLS.

TWEDDLE HALL, State, corner North Pearl.
ASSOCIATION HALL, State, corner Broadway.

EXPRESS OFFICES.

AMERICAN AND MERCHANTS' UNION, Broadway, corner Steuben.
ALBANY AND NEW YORK, Exchange Building, State street.
NATIONAL, 13 Exchange Building, State street.

TELEGRAPH OFFICES.

WESTERN UNION, State, corner Broadway. Branch Offices —Delavan House, Union Depot, West Albany, and State Capitol.
ATLANTIC AND PACIFIC, 463 Broadway.

NEWSPAPERS.

Albany Argus, Broadway, corner Beaver. Daily, semi-weekly and weekly.
Albany Evening Journal, 61 State. Daily, semi-weekly and weekly.
Albany Daily Knickerbocker, 1½ Green street.
Albany Evening Post, 7 Hudson street.
Albany Evening Times, 41 Hudson street.
Albany Morning Express, 52 State street.
Cultivator and Country Gentleman, 395 Broadway. Weekly.
Freie Blaetter, 44 Beaver street. Daily.
The Sunday Morning Press, No. 1 Green street. Weekly.

Watkins' House!

EUROPEAN PLAN.

No. 100 State Street, Albany.

☞ STRANGERS visiting the city, will find a First-Class RESTAURANT attached to the house.

COOPER HOUSE,

OTSEGO LAKE,

Cooperstown, N. Y.

☞ POPULAR SUMMER RESORT.

WILL OPEN JUNE 1st,

For the Season of 1870.

CHARLES A. WATKINS, Prop'r.

www.ingramcontent.com/pod-product-compliance
Lightning Source LLC
Chambersburg PA
CBHW020322090426

42735CB00009B/1364

*9 7 8 3 3 3 7 0 2 0 4 8 4 *